Be Happy

POWERFUL PROMPTS
FOR PERSONAL GROWTH & WELL-BEING

A JOURNAL

ROCK
POINT

INTRODUCTION

This journal is in your hands for a reason. Maybe it's because you refuse to settle for a mediocre form of happiness. Maybe you are thirsty for techniques that can boost your daily well-being. Maybe you could do with a moment to yourself to work on your quality of life, rather than caring for someone else all the time. Or maybe you received this journal from someone who cares about you.

However it ended up in your possession, this journal invites you into the global conversation on happiness and how we can create more of it. Here you will explore some of the strategies that have been found most effective for boosting your sense of happiness and well-being.

HOW TO USE THIS JOURNAL

You've probably already figured out that this journal is about fostering habits for happiness. But before we move on, let's clarify what is meant by happiness.

Happiness itself is an emotional state, and as emotional states go, it's fickle and impermanent, especially when you want it most. In this journal, you'll explore the broader concept of well-being, the one that includes all the ingredients you need to feel an overall sense of happiness.

Psychologist, educator, and author Martin Seligman's theory of flourishing includes the following components:

A) Positive emotions;
B) Activities that provide a sense of engagement (or flow);
C) Healthy relationships;
D) A sense of meaning and purpose; and
E) A sense of accomplishment.

From this list alone, you can see that it's not as simple as just becoming happy and then holding onto that pleasant emotional state with a white-knuckled grip. The good news is that you have a great deal of control over these happiness ingredients, and this journal will encourage your inner control freak and show you just how to take your ability to thrive into your own hands.

Of course, there are aspects of your own happiness that are not within your control. Professor and author Sonja Lyubomirsky's happiness pie chart divides the contributing factors to happiness into pieces.

First, you can't control your genetics; you have a predetermined set point for happiness. The combination of your personality and your genetic makeup account for 50 percent of your happiness. Second (and here's the kicker), the things we think will contribute to our happiness don't actually do much for our overall well-being. The vacation house with the private beach, the sports car you've always dreamed of owning—these things contribute to a measly 10 percent of your happiness. On top of that, any new possession or positive change in your circumstances (e.g., a pay raise) only changes happiness in the short term because of how adaptive we are as human beings.

You can win the lotto and, thanks to a process called "hedonic adaptation," end up just as happy (or unhappy) as you were before your bank account swelled, because you adapted to your new circumstances.

The good news is that the final piece of the happiness pie is large and controllable. That's right: you control at least 40 percent of your own happiness through your own choices and actions. As you make your way through this journal of self-discovery, you'll discern exactly which actions are going to shift you from simply surviving to all-out thriving.

If you're a fan of "fast"—not necessarily in the quick-fix kind of way, but in a this-fits-easily-into-my-day kind of way, then this journal (and journey!) is for you. A hardworking set of tools that you can access on your own terms, in your own time

This journal is organized into nine sections, each one asking you to choose an important part of living a full life, and determine how you may or may not have been doing so thus far. As you go through the prompts, you may find that you are following the right path. If that is the case,

think deeper on how you can push yourself further; there's always room for improvement. If this has not been your path, use the prompts as hardworking tools to map a new path to success, and make a deep commitment to changing your way of thinking.

The prompts in this journal will focus on diving deep into your personal power, the power you have in choosing emotional states and values that help you to live a full life based on what's important to you deep down.

You'll be encouraged to put these lessons to work and look at ways you can cement positivity into your everyday life. After taking time to look inward while answering these prompts and identifying which parts of your life you'd like to change, focus your energy toward making an actual difference.

Congratulations on acknowledging that you can get more out of life. The happiness habits you cultivate will show you how. Let's go!

Happiness is a transient emotional state—it can be hard to find, and harder still to hold onto for long. Some days, it may disappear for no good reason at all and leave you scrambling for other emotions to fill its place. Luckily, thriving is a psychological state that doesn't just rely on positive feelings like happiness, but on the daily choices we make. Want to live a rich, vital, fulfilling life? Choose your focus. Choose your actions.

Take some time to reflect on the choices you are currently making versus the choices you will be prompted to write about and explore. Sometimes our choices are unconscious, and it's not until we are presented with alternatives that we realize we've been sabotaging ourselves all along. We must think about the daily choices that determine (a) the emotional states we want to embody, and (b) the personal values we can connect with along the way.

Choosing Joy

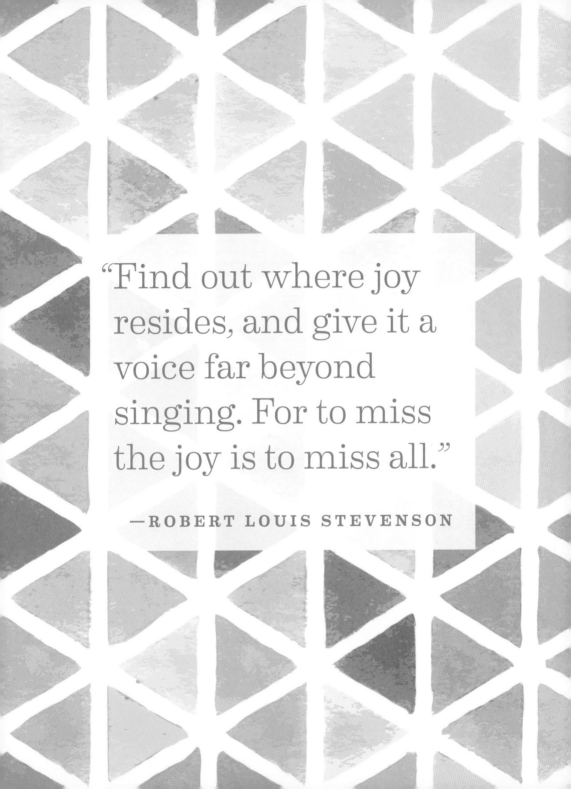

"Find out where joy resides, and give it a voice far beyond singing. For to miss the joy is to miss all."

—ROBERT LOUIS STEVENSON

We are blessed with the capacity to feel all the "colors" of the emotional rainbow, but too often we miss the brightest one. Joy, like all strong feelings, brings us closer to our true selves.

Our brains are problem-solving machines, designed to identify threats and keep us safe. They are not designed to revel in the bounty of tiny happy things that make the world beautiful. It's easy for the small joys to slip out of our grasp quickly, or pass by unnoticed altogether.

Our innate brain wiring is why we're unable to focus on positive things all the time. But we don't have to remain fixed in a negative emotional state because of that. We can deepen our experience of joy by focusing on the things that bring delight into our lives when they occur. A cool breeze on warm skin. An unexpected phone call from your best friend. A warm interaction with a stranger on the train. It doesn't matter what the situation is, and it doesn't matter what "brand" of joy it is— delight, elation, contentment, bliss, gladness. What matters is that we stop to notice it, embrace it, and celebrate it.

We can choose joy by savoring it. Joy is magnified when we savor the things that make us happy, no matter how small or large those things may be. But savoring requires you to be present. You need to be connected to the moment to drink it in, not stuck in the past or worried about the future (no easy feat, I know). Research has shown that we benefit from directly experiencing a moment as it is without viewing it through all the past experiences, memories, beliefs, and judgments that we carry through our lives. By mindfully savoring positive experiences, we can prolong and intensify positive feelings—and who doesn't want that?

Moments of joy enter our lives through many different kinds of vessels. A compliment from a friend, encouragement from a boss, the offering of a seat on the train by a stranger after a long day. Who are those who bring you joy through their actions?

It's important to show your joy.

Smile, pump your fist, do a backflip somewhere that has a soft landing, shake your rump . . . whatever does it for you! How will you express your joy today?

Whether it's your happy moment

or someone else's, take time to celebrate it. How will you celebrate
what brings you and those you love joy?

Keep a Joy List

When times get difficult (and they will), you can draw from this list
when you need a dose of delight in your day.

LIST FIVE joyful major life events:

LIST FIVE joyful everyday moments:

LIST FIVE joyful personal experiences:

LIST FIVE things or people that bring you joy:

Unless you make an occasion of things that are worth celebrating, they will generally pass you by—along with their significance in the progress of your life. What are some upcoming moments you want to take note to celebrate?

When someone asks you how you are, or how your day

was, remember to talk about the tiny happy things. What are the little things that brought you joy today?

Is there something in your life that you do not yet

possess that you truly believe will bring you great joy? Write about the
circumstances why you do not have it and chart a path for how you might
achieve it in a healthy way.

Choosing Gratitude

"When I started counting my blessings, my whole life turned around."

—WILLIE NELSON

If I were asked to name the most life-altering tool for ongoing happiness, it would be choosing to focus on gratitude. We live in a culture that constantly sends us messages of "not enough," selling us on the idea that we need more to be happy—more possessions, more money, more friends, more likes on social media. For all of the conveniences that the Internet gives us, it also gives us countless avenues for feelings of inadequacy by making us constantly compare ourselves to others whom we believe to be happier than we are because they only posted the good moments from their vacation.

Gratitude does the opposite: It puts us at peace with what is. It allows us to revel in what we already have by not overlooking it for something shinier in the distance. In other words, gratitude is the birthplace of enough, and enough is the birthplace of contentment.

Let's be real here: being in a state of "not enough" is automatic for most of us now. But the way out of the disease is in front of you, beside you, and within you.

Life with a gratitude habit helps counteract negative feelings such as jealousy, resentment, and entitlement. Holding a deep appreciation for where we are on our journey, the people around us, and the things we've collected along the way helps us shift from stressed to calm, from self-focused to other focused, and from pessimism to optimism.

So, how do we choose gratitude? We choose it with intention, with diligence, and with acceptance that it won't always change our moments in the short term, but it will transform our lives in the long run.

Make a list of the things you are grateful for.

Having a tangible record for you to reflect upon will become a fountain of gratitude when you need a reminder of what there is to be thankful for in your world.

Focus on the people around you.

How do you show gratitude for the kindness you receive from them?

How do others show their gratitude towards you?

What are the big, obvious good things
you are grateful for?

Name a few small, incidental things

that strike up gratitude within you.

We experience frustrations every day. Don't keep those emotions inside. Take the time to vent about your day and everything that went wrong.

Now write about what you're thankful for.

What made you feel grateful today?

Choosing Kindness

"It really shocks me when I encounter people who think kindness doesn't matter. Because I think it's pretty much the only thing that matters."

—JOSH RADNOR

Believing in kindness is the most important choice we can make in a world that gives us so many excuses to be cruel. Believe in kindness for the greater good, but also for the way it fortifies our relationships with others, from the people closest to our hearts to members of our communities we'll never meet. Choosing kindness is choosing connectedness.

Kindness is a surefire way to feel good. Doing something for someone else, especially if it takes some effort on your behalf, is action for happiness—both yours and theirs. Share the love and it's not just others who will benefit, it's the person doing the love sharing too. Kind people feel happier. And this only continues the cycle: Increase your happiness and you're likely to be kinder too.

Kindness holds hands with gratitude. One encourages the other. When we are consciously grateful for the kindness bestowed on us by someone else, it sparks a pay-it-forward cycle. On days when you're not feeling all that sunny emotionally, start with gratitude. Gratitude is the grounding force that will remind you of what's good (no matter how small) and lift you up so that you're able to pass that goodness onto others. Not being kind is difficult when you're already feeling grateful.

Kindness to others is important, but it's almost impossible to be authentically kind to others if you are being unkind to yourself. You count. Acting like you don't is not moving you any closer to happiness. Be mindful of the way you speak to yourself, the time you give yourself to enjoy life, and the amount of time you rest and recuperate. Self-kindness will only increase your kindness towards others and will lead you to go out into the world with a softer, more open approach. Keep your eyes open and you'll see no shortage of opportunities for kindness that the world is offering you.

Sometimes, the most powerful acts of kindness are

the ones that no one knows about except the recipient, who may or may not know you as the source. What acts of kindness have you done anonymously?

Random acts of kindness may seem spontaneous,

so make an effort to find space for them in your life.

LIST THREE acts of kindness you will do in one day:

LIST THREE acts of kindness you will do over one week:

LIST THREE acts of kindness you will do over one month:

LIST THREE acts of kindness you will do over one year:

Loved ones are easy to take for granted.

Was there ever a time you failed show kindness to a constant in your life?

How can you make a difference to those people
who make a difference to you just by being part of your world?

Kindness happens internally as much as externally.

Why do you deserve kindness?

Speak kindly to yourself.

LIST FIVE kind phrases you can say about yourself:

Use encouraging words

LIST FIVE inspiring phrases you can reflect on when you need a push to keep going:

Give yourself time to rest.

BRAINSTORM FIVE ways you will give your body,
mind and soul the opportunity to rest:

Remind yourself you are worthy

CREATE FIVE affirmations you can tell yourself daily:

Choosing Patience

"The key to everything is patience. You get the chicken by hatching the egg, not by smashing it."

—ARNOLD H. GLASOW

We can't speak about happiness unless we cover those things that are the most important contributors to happiness, even when those things require a significant degree of effort. You have to be patient with patience.

It's all too easy to be swept up in the speed of life. We all have tendencies to decide what we want to do or where we want to go and then wanting to be there instantaneously. On good days, we might accept a minimum amount of effort before we lapse back into impatient desires to be there/be done/have arrived.

So, what? Buying into the need to hustle to get happier, make your dreams come true, find love, or get to work on time feeds into the fear system in our brains. It feeds the idea of scarcity and convinces us that there's not enough of everything to go around. It feeds the idea that rest is only for the weak. And the urgency this creates is a trigger for surviving, but not for thriving. When we are in survival mode, our bodies are flooded with stress hormones such as cortisol and adrenaline— hormones that cloud our creativity, tangle our thoughts, and convince us that we have very few options for solving the problems sitting in front of us.

This is not to say that we shouldn't work hard. Working hard in a lifestyle that also includes rest, play, and reasonable time for the general demands of daily life will nourish your mind, heart, and soul so much more than "rise and grind" ever will.

But how do we do this in a culture that warns us that we risk our very worth as humans if we stop to catch our breath? The answer is tough but necessary: We choose patience. We choose to step back, to take full and complete breaths, and to reject the idea that things don't get done unless we rush at and through them. We choose patience for the times we don't get it right and the times obstacles show up. And we choose to forgive ourselves when we default to rushing because we buy into keeping up with the crowd and fitting in.

Patience is a mindset as much as it is an emotional state. It's a value and a way of being. It's important to note that you can work hard and choose patience. You can follow your dreams and choose patience. You can be healing and patient. And you can be patient in all the roles you fulfill daily: partner, parent, child, sibling, friend, colleague, teammate, grandparent.

Become aware of racing thoughts and racing actions.

Make a choice to give up the rush for a period of time. What are a few small choices you can make to slow down?

Now think about the big picture.

What are some life adjusting changes you can make to start slow living every day?

Rushing through life has consequences—

some can be amazing and others devastating. When were some times that being speedy benefited you?

What are some times

where the outcomes were not so great?

What has changed in your life
to make you not so patient?

What are some situations
that require you to have infinite reserves of patience?

For one day, keep your phone in your pocket,

and take your watch off. You don't have to check the time every five minutes to know what you need to do next. At the end of the day, journal about your experience.

What did you notice about the world
once you stop worrying about time?

How were your interactions with those around you?

How did you feel internally during the day?

Were you more or less productive?

Trust that life is happening as it needs to right now.

Trust yourself to do what you need to do in order to create the life you want to live, without compromising your wellbeing in the process. Imagine a day where you did nothing but just relaxed with yourself. Write down your self-care goals for that day.

Choosing Laughter

"Life is worth living
as long as there's a
laugh in it."

—L. M. MONTGOMERY

The relationship between humor and happiness is fundamental. Being able to see the funny side of life helps us cope when life doesn't go our way. It helps us to manage the relentless problem-solving machines that are our brains by interjecting reasons to not take life all that seriously. Yes, we are wired to focus on everything that has gone wrong and will go wrong. What we are less likely to do is to find a way to see the positive, even ridiculous, side to difficult situations.

Humor can be protective. It can enable people to keep doing their jobs in situations that can only be described as horrendous. Humor can help people heal and talk through their problems by scaffolding the discussion with a joke to prevent things from getting too emotionally heavy too quickly. Humor is the light in our lives. It interrupts the shadows of our problems, even just momentarily, to brings us back into the light.

However, choosing humor is not about laughing inappropriately in the face of pain. It's not about invalidating what's hurt you or laughing at another person's experience in a way that hurts or invalidates him or her. Choosing humor is about being able to step into a different perspective when it's possible and appropriate. Choosing humor is about changing the default lens through which we usually see life.

When you choose humor, you automatically experience an increase in pleasant feelings. But that doesn't mean that you have to be a comedian about every part of your life. No, it means that you can find the playful side of yourself, the side that can razz and banter, rib and gag. It's about the choice you have to give up the business side of life for a minute and remember that you don't need permission to have fun.

And if you needed another reason to look on the funny side, humor is a bonding agent. It brings us closer together. You know that person who gets you? You probably feel that way because they laugh at the same things you do. You share the same humor dialect. And when things get tough, that person is often just as medicinal as any other alternative you have available. Side note: We usually have people in our lives that play different roles. We need the person who listens to the pain and gives a piece of sage advice as much as we need the person who makes us laugh until our bellies hurt. Sometimes this might be the same person, sometimes not. Be open to your friends and their strengths. They will shine at different times and for different reasons.

Think about a tough situation you have been in.

Was there a funny side to it?

Will you look back on this and laugh?

Can you laugh at it now?

Who are the people in your life who show you the funny side?

Write about three funny incidents or moments from your day.

Think about the last time you laughed.

Like, really laughed. What were the positive feelings that came with that laughter?

Think about your week.

What were three small but hilarious things that might have gone unnoticed in the moment, but you find yourself thinking back on and smiling?

Name five people who make you laugh.
and what you like most about them.

_____

_____

_____

_____

_____

Name five people you can count on
to help you see the lighter side when you can't do so for yourself.

_____

_____

_____

_____

_____

Think about the types of people you don't have in your life

but would like to. Describe them here and how you might seek them out
to make them part of your tribe.

What can you do to help them in times of need?

Choosing the Bright Side

"Optimists are right. So are pessimists. It's up to you to choose which you will be."

—HARVEY MACKAY

If there is any topic on which your inherent choice needs to be emphasized, it is choosing to look on the optimistic side of events rather than on the pessimistic side. It's true that our brains have a bias towards negativity, thanks to the pesky need to focus on survival that we inherited from our ancestors. This means that it's natural to focus on problems. It's natural for our minds to first point out the things that aren't working, or our flaws and mistakes, or the obstacles in front of our goals. What's not usually automatic is looking towards the brighter side of how things might work out.

Your sense of happiness and contentment will grow when you focus your energies on things turning out for the better (perhaps not always the best, but for the better) in the long run. And when things go wrong, optimism strengthens your capacity to be able to cope, recover, and rebuild.

Whether your viewpoint is optimistic or pessimistic depends on three ways you interpret negative events: A) Do you tend to assume that horrible circumstances or feelings are here to stay, or do you remind yourself that they will pass and give way to better days? B) Do you tend to view negative things as all-encompassing, as taking up your entire life and defining your entire character, or are you able to view those things in balance with the positive things/characteristics that are also present? C) Do you take negative things personally and turn the blame upon yourself, or do you attribute negative things to factors outside of yourself?

The direction in which you interpret negative and positive events has a considerable impact on your approach to life overall. Being able to turn toward the bright side of life by choice, and with full acknowledgment that there is effort involved, helps us to move towards thriving. It's a choice we make, even when our typical state might be to focus on the negative. Our default states can even change over time, if we take the time to practice new ways of thinking that eventually rewire our brains.

Why would you bother, though? If it's difficult to do, why would you add the extra effort to your life when you might already be struggling to simply get through the day? Because healthy well-being is a project that takes an entire lifetime, and because you're here trying to improve yourself. A choice toward optimism is a choice towards your future happiness.

Think about the last time you were in a seemingly
dire situation. At the time, was there a positive side to be found?

Can you look back on that incident
and see now that there was a bright side?

Brainstorm some ways you can make a habit
of staying positive for the future.

Who in your life could show me the bright side
when things seem bleak?

Pick an area of your life that is a priority for you

Take at least ten minutes to journal about this area of your life working out exactly as you dreamed it would be. If everything went your way, and dreams came true, what would it look like? Do this for as many life areas as need them.

Take a moment to look back on times when you entered

into a negative place. (I know, it hurts. But trust me, there's a reason for it.) Now think of how things actually turned out. Was it as bad as you thought it would be?

And if it was bad at the time, what did it bring

into your life that was ultimately good for your well-being? A special person?
A new perspective? A lesson learned?

When are the times you naturally feel like an optimist.

pessimist, or realist? It's normal to cycle through these states of being and is healthy to be a little of each given the situation.

Choosing
Courage

"Courage starts
with showing
up and letting
ourselves be seen."

—BRENÉ BROWN

You don't have to go far to find an inspirational quote on courage accompanied by the requisite picture of a majestic lion or a guy with a barrel chest standing on top of a mountain. It's a frame of mind that has been packaged so much that we sometimes need a reminder that scrolling by a quote on courage in your Instagram feed and sharing it because you wholeheartedly agree with it is not the same thing as taking a courageous action.

You don't need to be climbing mountains, or even "doing one thing every day that scares you" (unless that's your jam, of course). But living courageously requires us to do something. It is just as much about the quiet, unseen decisions that we make daily as it is about confronting the bigger goals we set throughout our lives. You see, courage is not present when life is easy. It doesn't have to be. We don't need courage to go to the store to get some milk, or get ready for work, or vacuum the floor (motivation, yes, but not courage). And we don't need courage to hear positive feedback about how we're doing, or to take stock of our lives when everything seems to be in its place. We need courage when things get hard. When we want to give up but need to keep going. We need courage when we fail or make a mistake. And when life delivers us a set of circumstances we did not order during our last online shopping spree. There's a common misconception that courage occurs independently in its own right. It doesn't. Courage doesn't show up unless you need it. So, if you keep yourself safe from emotional discomfort, wrapped up and warm until courage appears so that you may go ahead and truly start living, you may be waiting a very long time and find that you are stuck before you've even started.

You see, courage is right there beside you when fear is loudest, rejection is nipping at your heels, and shame is ready to parade you naked to the world. Courage shows up when we know the risks but we do it anyway. When we say to ourselves that living authentically is more important than staying comfortable. That's where you'll find courage. And courage is contagious. So, you know that thing you have to give to the world? Please put it out there. Please take the step and trust that courage will show up. Doing so is the only way that we live fully, richly and deeply, and doing so is the greatest gift you can give yourself and the people around you. Choose to live with courage and authenticity, because that's true beauty.

What type of situations make you uncomfortable?

What type of situations make you feel fear?

What inspires you to take courageous action
when the going gets tough?

_____

_____

_____

_____

_____

What emotions enable you to accept and embrace
discomfort and fear and ultimately help you find your courage?

_____

_____

_____

_____

_____

Think about the last time you were courageous.

Why did you put aside your fear and were able to power forward?

Write about a time you needed courage in order to heal

a personal wound, whether spiritual, emotional or physical.

Write about a time you needed courage because
someone needed you even when you didn't think you were ready.

Write about a time when life has disrupted your plans

when didn't know how you'd face tomorrow, let alone where you were headed next,
but you drew on your courage to show you the way.

Write about a time when you were forced
to expand your comfort zone.

Choosing Self-Love

"You have been criticizing yourself for years, and it hasn't worked. Try approving of yourself and see what happens."

—LOUISE L. HAY

Perhaps your Internal Board of Criticism is already holding a meeting about the title of this section. Perhaps its members are already warning you that self-love is simply some gimmick for the Soft Ones and that the only thing you need is to be reminded of your faults and all the ways that you don't measure up to help you stay on the straight and narrow. You probably have had years of practice listening to your Internal Board of Criticism. And where has it gotten you? Has it ever actually helped?

Probably not. Instead, the scolding and repri-manding that those inner voices have tossed your way have only served to keep you stuck in patterns of self-sabotage, of procrastination, of I'll-do-it-someday and only-when-I'm-good enough. Those voices are so automatic by now that you don't always know when they are speaking, or at the very best, you listen to them because you are convinced that it's in your best interest to do so, because it will make you a better version of whatever it is that you're trying to be.

That's nonsense. There is no amount of self-criticism that has ever helped someone on their way to better well-being. And just so we're clear, this is not about admitting when you've made a mistake and resolving to do better next time. It's about the chatter that constantly tells you that you are not the right dress size or weight, or pretty enough, or smart enough, or important enough, or rich enough, or good enough on any level. These are the voices that tell you you're a bad parent, son, sister, friend, employee, business owner, or person in general. You don't choose these voices. These voices are just there. But you have another option and that is to choose self-love. To choose to reform your relationship with yourself. To start treating yourself like you are worthy, valuable, and worth taking care of.

It's not easy to overcome default thought or behavior patterns. But with conscious awareness, you can befriend yourself—and then watch as your well-being, productivity, confidence, and general happiness bloom!

What are your personal strengths?

What are the things that you like about yourself?

Check in with your needs and respect them.

Do what needs to be done to respect yourself. Write down a list of your needs.
Be honest with yourself about them.

How are you currently getting your needs met?

Is it through activities, a person, a place?

Who in your life is your champion when

self-criticism creeps in? What are some things they say to you that you can draw on
to build up your confidence in low moments?

Think about the last negative thing you said about yourself.

Would you speak to a friend like this?

In what situation, if any,

would you treat a friend negatively?

If you acted like this towards a friend,

would that person feel good about themselves?

If you acted like this toward a friend,

would they be motivated to move forward with their life?

Choosing Flow

"It is by being fully involved with every detail of our lives, whether good or bad, that we find happiness—not by trying to look for it directly."

—MIHALY CSIK SZENTMIHALYI

Flow is that pleasant state of being so completely absorbed in an activity that you lose your sense of time. It's the mental state characterized by sharpened focus for an activity that brings you into the "zone"—the place where you are engrossed in what you are doing in an enjoyable, motivational way. We have an ambivalent relationship with flow. This is a great state, but, by nature, we don't love effort of any kind, and the idea that we have to put in effort to get to flow makes us wonder whether or not it's really worth it. But unless you show up in the first place, flow won't find you.

When was the last time you did something that absorbed your attention to the point of losing time? To the point that you were so engaged in the activity that you experienced your world in macro view, zooming in on just your space, your moment, your thing?

Flow is a feeding tube to happiness. Do more things that help you access this mental state and you'll nourish your well-being. Often the problem is that we don't give ourselves the time to do the things that invite flow. And often, it's the initial effort that we are quick to reject, with excuses of "can't be bothered" or "do it later." And before we know it, we are caught up in doing too many of the have-to activities and not enough of the want-to activities.

For you, it might be a creative pursuit, such as painting or playing music. Perhaps it's rock climbing, running, reading, or planning your next home renovation. Whatever it is, the activity is about what it brings you. It's an interaction of mindful effort with the reward of the activity itself.

Please be aware that if it's an activity like social media scrolling or phone gaming, it might not be the flow you're looking for. These activities can at times be cathartic and entertaining, but they can quickly become an absorption that is out of balance with the other aspects of your life. When referring to flow here, we're talking about the activities that add to your well-being, rather than ones that deaden your awareness because of their addictive qualities, which cause you to ignore other areas of your life.

Write about five activities or experiences
you normally lump into multi-tasking but that you want to focus on completely.

What do you do that engages you completely

and pleases you infinitely? These are the activities that get you into a state of flow.

If you're at a point in your life where you

aren't doing anything like that for yourself, think back to a time when you were. What were those activities? When did you do them? What did they look like?

Commit to five minutes of a chosen activity in which you
focus solely on that activity. Do exactly what mindfulness masters do: when your
attention wanders, gently bring it back to the task. Journal about your experience.

What are a few of your daily responsibilities
that command most of your time?

Which of those responsibilities can you hand off
to another or ask for assistance with?

What are some ways you
can prioritize your well-being?

How can you use your "me time" effectively?

Think of some times where you have self-sabotaged.

How could these have been avoided?

What are the main reasons
you fall victim to procrastination?

List ten realistic and manageable things

you can do to escape the pressures of daily life and regain a sense of self.

CONCLUDING WISHES

Forming habits for happiness takes effort and goes beyond just feeling good. It's about breaking your routine and making an effort, every day, to be the person you want to be. Hopefully, this journal has added value to your daily life. May you prioritize your well-being, because your life depends on it! Don't settle for merely existing when you can grow, thrive, and be happy. You can do this!

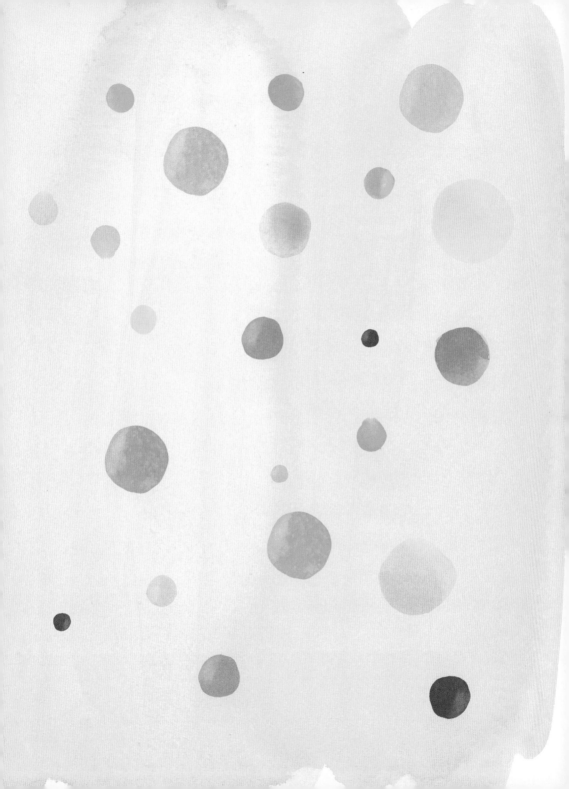

Inspiring | Educating | Creating | Entertaining

Brimming with creative inspiration, how-to projects, and useful information to enrich your everyday life, Quarto Knows is a favorite destination for those pursuing their interests and passions. Visit our site and dig deeper with our books into your area of interest: Quarto Creates, Quarto Cooks, Quarto Homes, Quarto Lives, Quarto Drives, Quarto Explores, Quarto Gifts, or Quarto Kids.

10 9 8 7 6 5 4 3 2 1

ISBN: 978-1-63106-743-3

Publisher: Rage Kindelsperger
Creative Director: Laura Drew
Managing Editor: Cara Donaldson
Cover: Cindy Samargia Laun
Interior Layout: Beth Middleworth

This journal provides general information and guides on forming positive habits. It does not provide any medical information regarding mental or emotional health. The author and publisher are in no way responsible for any actions of behaviors undertaken by the user of this journal.

Printed in China